RACING SUPERCARS

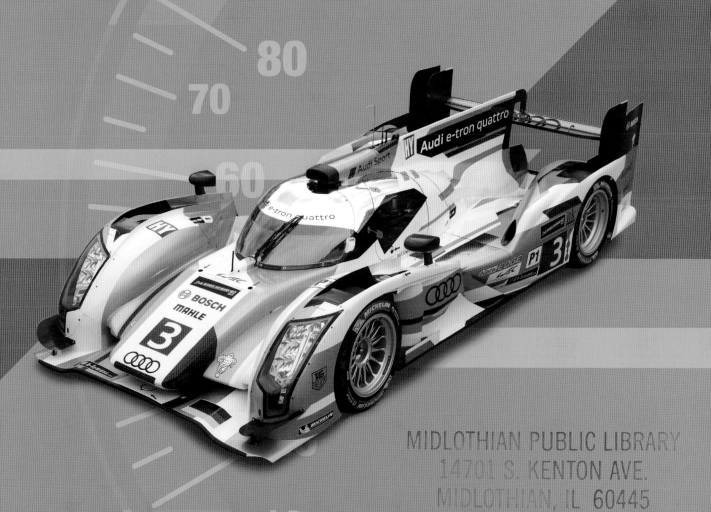

PAUL HARRISON

ARCTURUS

First published in 2015 by Arcturus Publishing

Distributed by Black Rabbit Books.

P. O. Box 3263
Mankato
Minnesota MN 56002

Printed in China

Cataloging-in-Publication Data is available from the Library of Congress
ISBN: 978-1-78404-075-8

Text: Paul Harrison
Editor: Joe Harris
Assistant editor: Frances Evans
Design: sprout.uk.com
Cover design: sprout.uk.com
Picture research: Mirco De Cet

Picture credits:
Audi UK: cover, 28-29, 28b, 29r. Bradhall71: 16b. Corbis: 30 (HOCH ZWEI/Thomas Suer/dpa), 14 (Transtock). General Motors: contents, 20-21. Gsenkow: 6-7. Shutterstock: 10-11, 26 (Rodrigo Garrido), 25tr (Art Konovalov), 19, 31 (Luis Louro), 18 (Julie Lucht), 24-25 (Jason Meredith), 4-5 (Natursports), 22-23 (Martin Preston), 8-9 (PhotoStock10), 12-13 (Philip Rubino), 27 (Christian Vinces). Transtock/SuperStock: 15. UNSW Solar Car Racing Team—Sunswift: 16t, 17.

SL004073US

Supplier 29, Date 0514, Print run 3418

CONTENTS

FERRARI F138

What makes a racing supercar super? Most racing cars are designed with one feature in mind—the ability to reach incredible speeds and win races! The Ferrari F138 is the most high-tech racing car on the track. This is the result of spending millions of dollars and many years on the car's design and testing.

The car's chassis is made from carbon fiber, which is both light and very strong. The carbon fiber is made in a honeycomb design to further reduce weight.

The large hole above the driver's head is an air intake. This diverts air toward the engine to keep it cool.

Flaps on the rear spoilers open and close to boost the car's speed.

Big tires give the car lots of grip on the race track.

The F138 was developed in a wind tunnel—a machine that shows designers how the air is flowing around the car. The more easily the air moves, the faster the car will go.

The Formula 1 World Championship is the world's most glamorous motor race series. To win it in 2013, Ferrari had to try to improve on the previous season's car. The rules about what teams can do to their cars change each season. So Ferrari designers were trying to get the best car they could while staying within the rules. The result was the F138.

The F138 has seven forward gears and one reverse gear.

Spoilers on the front and back of the car use air to push the car to the track and give it extra grip.

SUPER STATS

FERRARI F138

TOP SPEED: Top secret but over 185 mph (300 km/h)

0–60 MPH (0-97 KM/H) : Top secret but under 3 seconds

HORSEPOWER: Top secret

LENGTH: 178.9 in (4,545 mm)

WIDTH: 70.7 in (1,796 mm)

HEIGHT: 37.7 in (959 mm)

MADE IN: Italy

TOP FUEL
FUNNY CAR

"Funny Cars" are no joke! They are a type of long, narrow drag racing car. And their lightning speeds and incredible acceleration are no laughing matter. In fact, in a straight race, a Funny Car would leave a Formula 1 car standing. That's because it is one of the fastest racing cars around.

The only cars faster than the Funny Cars are called Top Fuel Rails. These are longer, skinnier dragsters that have their engines at the back for better grip.

Many Funny Cars have no doors: instead the body of the car lifts up for the driver to get in.

The chassis is made from carbon fiber, a strong but lightweight material.

Massive back wheels are needed to provide enough grip and to cope with all the power the engine produces.

In a drag race, two dragsters race side by side over a short track. The race track measures 0.25 miles (0.4 km). There are different types of dragster, with the Top Fuel cars being the fastest. Typically, a Top Fuel car will finish the race in under 4 seconds!

Top Fuel cars don't use normal fuel but a mixture of gasoline and nitro methane. This fuel provides more power to the engine.

Not all the fuel is burned in the engine. Some burns up in the exhaust, shooting red-hot flames out of the back.

Nitro methane might add more power, but it's an expensive fuel to buy and dragsters use lots of it. A Top Fuel Funny Car can use around a gallon (3.6 l) in a second!

SUPER STATS

TOP FUEL FUNNY CAR
TOP SPEED: More than 300 mph (483 km/h)
0–60 MPH (0-97 KM/H) : Under 1 second
HORSEPOWER: Over 7,000 bhp
LENGTH: Varies from car to car
WIDTH: Varies from car to car
HEIGHT: Varies from car to car
MADE IN: Mainly USA

7

DRIFT RACING

Drift racing is different from most car racing. It's not about how fast you can go, but how good you are at skidding and spinning! The sport started in Japan in the 1960s and drifting competitions are now held worldwide. Models such as the Nissan 200SX and the Mazda RX-7 FD35 are considered to be some of the best drift racing cars.

Big clouds of smoke billow out from the back wheels as the car squeals and slides around the race track at lightning speed.

Drift racing cars usually have a rear-wheel drive, which means the power from the engine goes to the back wheels, not the front.

The engine in a drift racer is turbo-charged. This means it has a system that increases the power that the engine can produce, making the car faster.

Drift racing uses the skills of the driver to get the car into a controlled sideways slide as it travels around the race track. This may not be the fastest way of getting round the race track, but that's not the point. Instead, drivers get points for how well they control the slide. Cars often compete, one on one against each other in knockout tournaments.

A drift racer needs to control the car's accelerator, clutch, and brake pedals, as well as keeping an eye on the car's speed and steering.

Although there are drifting races all around the world, the sport is not controlled by the FIA (Federation Internationale de l'Automobile). The FIA is the organization that oversees most forms of professional motor sport.

SUPER STATS

DRIFT RACER *(The following stats relate to a Nissan 200SX)*

TOP SPEED: 146 mph (235 km/h)

0–60 MPH (0-97 KM/H) : 7 seconds

HORSEPOWER: 197 bhp

LENGTH: 178 in (4,521 mm)

WIDTH: 68.1 in (1,731 mm)

HEIGHT: 51 in (1,296 mm)

MADE IN: Japan

VOLKSWAGEN
POLO R WRC

The Volkswagen Polo may be the hatchback car favored by grannies the world over, but it's unlikely your granny has ever been behind the wheel of the R WRC version of the Volkswagen Polo. That's because this is a top-level rally car, designed to compete in some of the toughest racing conditions going.

Unlike most cars involved in motor sports, rally cars are designed to seat two people—a driver and a navigator who directs the driver using a map. No GPS here!

The R WRC's engine is a lot more powerful than the one found in a standard Polo.

Unlike the road-going version of the Polo, the rally version has had its back seats taken out and a support cage built inside for protection in the event of a crash. And in rallying, the chances of a crash are particularly high.

A large spoiler at the back of the car helps use the air flowing over the car to push the Polo downward, helping it to find grip on slippery surfaces.

Bigger, stronger brakes are needed to slow the car more quickly—otherwise the Polo would end up wrapped around a tree or in a ditch.

Rally car races take place over a range of different road surfaces, varying from paved roads to gravel tracks to ice and snow. That's tough on any car, and to make it even harder the rules state that rally cars, such as the Polo, have to be based on models that the general public can buy. Imagine pulling out of your driveway in an R WRC!

The body of the car has to be specially reinforced to help it survive any hard knocks.

SUPER STATS

VOLKSWAGEN POLO R WRC
TOP SPEED: Around 125 mph (200 km/h)
0–60 MPH (0-97 KM/H) : Around 3.9 seconds
HORSEPOWER: 315 bhp
LENGTH: 156.5 in (3,976 mm)
WIDTH: 71.6 in (1,820 mm)
HEIGHT: 53.3 in (1,356 mm)
MADE IN: Germany

Rally cars may have small engines, but they can still reach speeds of around 125 mph (200 km/h).

PEUGEOT 208 T16

At first glance, the Peugeot 208 T16 looks just like any other rally car. But the T16 is a record-breaking racing machine, specially modified to take part in a unique type of race known as hill climbing. This Peugeot is super fast, super powerful, and super grippy—the ideal combination for conquering the unique conditions of hill climbing.

Speed is essential and it takes less than 2 seconds for the T16 to get from 0 mph to 60 mph (0–100 km/h)!

There are huge spoilers on the front and the back of the T16 to push the car down onto the road surface for extra grip.

The chassis is made from lightweight carbon fiber panels over a strong tubular steel frame.

The rear spoiler was originally designed for a car that was meant to compete in 24-hour races such as the famous Le Mans event.

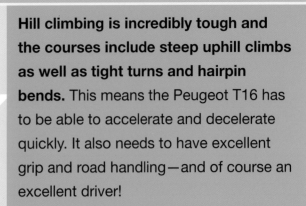

Hill climbing is incredibly tough and the courses include steep uphill climbs as well as tight turns and hairpin bends. This means the Peugeot T16 has to be able to accelerate and decelerate quickly. It also needs to have excellent grip and road handling—and of course an excellent driver!

In 2013 the T16 won the famous Pikes Peak hill climb race in the USA in record-breaking time.

The T16's wheel arches are bigger than a standard 208 car to allow larger wheels to be used. Bigger wheels mean bigger tires and bigger tires give more grip.

The T16's brakes are made from a material called carbon ceramic. They are lighter and give better results than standard metal brakes.

SUPER STATS

PEUGEOT 208 T16
TOP SPEED: 149 mph (240 km/h)
0–60 MPH (0-97 KM/H) : 1.8 seconds
HORSEPOWER: 875 bhp
LENGTH: 177.2 in (4,500 mm)
WIDTH: 78.7 in (2,000 mm)
HEIGHT: 51.2 in (1,300 mm)
MADE IN: France

MEAN MACHINES

SANDRAIL

Sandrails are the ultimate "build-it-yourself" racing supercars. These ultra-light specialist racers are the Frankenstein's monsters of the car racing world. Built from bits and pieces of other cars and held together with some DIY welding, they may not sound great, but nothing beats a sandrail for blasting across sand dunes.

Sandrails have very few body panels, which keeps their weight down.

Large tires help to spread the weight of the car better than small tires and prevent the car sinking into soft sand.

Sandrails get their name from the fact that the cars look like they have been made from long pieces of steel—which in fact they have!

The rear tires have large, evenly spaced ridges, known as paddles, for extra grip on the slippery sand.

Sandrails are sometimes called dune buggies, though strictly speaking dune buggies tend to be heavier and have more body panels.

Driving on sand is unlike traveling on any other surface, and it's something most cars can't do. That's what makes sandrails so amazing—not only can they drive over sand but they can race over the biggest dunes without getting stuck. That's down to the sandrail's power, light weight and specially designed tires.

Sandrails work well in extreme muddy conditions, too!

SUPER STATS

SANDRAIL *(All figures are just a guide as each sandrail will be different)*
TOP SPEED: 70 mph (113 km/h)
0–60 MPH (0-97 KM/H) : 7 seconds
HORSEPOWER: 68 bhp
LENGTH: 122 in (3,098 mm)
WIDTH: 84 in (2,134 mm)
HEIGHT: 60 in (1,524 mm)
MADE IN: USA

SUNSWIFT IV AND EVE

Imagine driving a car and never having to worry about fuel! Well, that dream is a reality with Sunswift IV. This supercar runs on the power of the Sun alone by converting energy from the Sun's rays into electricity that powers the car. As if this wasn't incredible enough, Sunswift IV is also a record breaker. It's the fastest solar-powered car on the planet!

The top, flat surface of the car is basically a large set of solar panels.

The Sunswift IV, nicknamed Ivy, has three narrow wheels. Big fat tires would cause more friction on the road which would slow the car down.

Sunswift IV is good for the environment because it doesn't cause any pollution. However, it's not good for passengers— there's only one seat!

The energy from the solar panels can be used to power the car or can be stored in a battery and used later.

The body is made from lightweight carbon fiber.

For the last couple of decades there have been competitions to produce the best solar-powered cars. Generally the cars, like Sunswift, are built by students and scientists trying to beat records for either speed or distance. The latest addition from Sunswift, called eVe, aims to look more like a traditional car. It has four wheels and there's room for both a driver and a passenger!

Cowlings around the front wheels help to make the car more aerodynamic.

SUPER STATS

SUNSWIFT IV
TOP SPEED: 70 mph (115 km/h)
0–60 MPH (0-97 KM/H): Not applicable
HORSEPOWER: Not applicable
LENGTH: 181 in (4,600 mm)
WIDTH: 70.8 in (1,800 mm)
HEIGHT: 70.8 in (1,800 mm)
MADE IN: USA

HONDA CIVIC NGTC

If you want extreme driving thrills from a run-of-the-mill family hatchback, then the Honda Civic NGTC is the car for you. This super-version of the family model takes part in the British Touring Car Championships and proves that big surprises—and big performances—can come in small packages!

The key to successful racing is speed, so the engine is more than twice as powerful as a standard Honda Civic—and accelerates twice as fast.

The engine costs around $40,000—more than enough to buy a brand new version of a normal Honda Civic, but cheap by motor racing standards!

A steel safety cage inside the car protects the driver in the event of a crash.

Skirting around the bottom of the car uses the air to increase grip.

The Civic belongs to a breed of racing car designed to satisfy the new rules of the British Touring Car Championship. In order to attract new teams to the competition, a new generation of cars, including the Honda Civic, is being produced that are much cheaper to build and run than before. Even so, it still costs around $300,000 to compete!

Crashes and collisions are common in touring car races so the Civic's fuel tank is protected by Kevlar—the same material that is used in bullet-proof jackets.

There are no creature comforts inside—even the inside door panels have been removed to save weight and reduce the risk of fire.

Although the Civic is a family car, there's no chance of taking the family with you—all the seats, apart from the driver's, have been removed.

SUPER STATS

HONDA CIVIC NGTC
TOP SPEED: 160 mph (257 km/h)
0–60 MPH (0-97 KM/H) : Top secret
HORSEPOWER: Over 300 bhp
LENGTH: Around 177 in (4,500 mm)
WIDTH: Around 70 in (1,770 mm)
HEIGHT: Around 62.9 in (1,600 mm)
MADE IN: Japan

CHEVROLET SS

The Chevrolet SS stands out in America's most popular form of motor sport, NASCAR. These supercars are based on cars that anyone can buy from a showroom. But there's nothing ordinary about the Chevrolet. From its massive engine to its mega-performance, the SS is a thoroughbred racer.

The car is heavier on one side than the other. This is to help the driver deal with the oval-shaped racing tracks with their steeply banked sides.

There are no side windows in the front doors so the driver can get out quickly in the event of an accident.

There have been a number of huge crashes in NASCAR races, so driver safety is important. The Chevrolet has a strong roll cage inside, with an thick extra support beam running through the middle of the car.

Special roof flaps pop up to stop the car from flipping over.

The Chevrolet SS is built to compete in grueling NASCAR races that can last for more 500 miles (800 km). To make it even harder, the races can take place on steeply banked tracks, which puts extra strain on the car and the driver.

Designers spend many hours testing the car in wind tunnels. They make sure air flows around the car properly to give maximum speed and grip.

In the event of an accident, the car is designed to push the engine downward rather than into the driver's legs.

The exhaust pipes are positioned on the right-hand side of the car, away from the driver, who sits on the left.

SUPER STATS

CHEVROLET SS
TOP SPEED: Top secret
0–60 MPH (0-97 KM/H) : Around 5 seconds
HORSEPOWER: Around 415 bhp
LENGTH: 200.4 in (5,090 mm)
WIDTH: 72.9 in (1,852 mm)
HEIGHT: 58.7 in (1,491 mm)
MADE IN: USA

BRISCA STOCK CAR

BriSCA stock cars are the bruisers of the supercar racing world. These near-indestructible race cars are allowed to push and shunt each other out of the way, which leads to real thrill and spill racing. And in stock car racing, the slower cars start at the front so if the fastest drivers want to win, they have to force their way to the front—it's brutal!

The massive wing on the top acts like a huge spoiler giving lots of grip around the corners.

The bumpers at the front are for pushing other cars out of the way—the ones at the back are for protecting the car from being hit from behind.

BriSCA cars can weigh no more than 3,200 lbs (1,450 kg) and you can have slightly more weight on one side to help it travel round the oval track.

Tires come under lots of pressure during stock car races, so they are made specially for this type of racing.

Not only do these cars have to contend with being bashed around, they also have a tricky race track to race round. Stock cars race around a 400 m (438 yard) oval track, so there's lots of steering involved. Plus, the surface of the tracks can be made of either tarmacadam or a loose gravel-like surface called shale, which offers less grip.

There's no limit to how big the BriSCA's engine can be. Teams have to get the right balance between using the most powerful engine they can without using one that is so heavy that it slows the car down.

Pete BARTRAM
913

861 BJS MOTORS

Side impact rails offer more protection for the car and driver.

As crashing and bashing is part of the sport, the cars have to be made from high-quality steel tubing to withstand the blows.

SUPER STATS

BRISCA STOCK CAR
TOP SPEED: Around 100 mph (160 km/h)
0–60 MPH (0-97 KM/H) : Around 4 seconds
HORSEPOWER: Around 600 bhp
LENGTH: Around 146 in (3,700 mm)
WIDTH: Around 73 in (1,850 mm)
HEIGHT: Around 54 in (1,370 mm)—
 not including roof wing
MADE IN: Great Britain

DEMOLITION DERBY

Without a shadow of a doubt, the worst-looking race cars around are those used in action-packed demolition derbies. This wacky group of beaten-up motor cars are having their last hurrah before visiting the scrap heap. And what better way to do it than in an extravaganza of motoring mayhem and destruction!

The original fuel tanks are removed and replaced with smaller, tougher tanks or wrapped in leak-proof material.

A basic roll cage is fitted to protect the driver in the highly likely event that the car gets badly damaged.

For safety reasons the car battery is moved inside the roll cage.

All of the glass and plastic is removed to stop any sharp bits injuring fellow drivers or spectators.

It's against the rules to add any new protective bumpers or to make the body of the car stronger than it was originally. Often bumpers are actually removed.

In a demolition derby, it's not your speed that counts—and to be honest these cars aren't particularly fast—but your ability to last. Cars are allowed to smash and bash into each other as they race around the circuit. The winner of the derby is the last car that is still able to move—smasharoo!

Doors have to be welded shut to stop them springing open mid-race.

Wheels have been known to come flying off—but that doesn't stop these cars. They just continue on three wheels!

SUPER STATS

DEMOLITION DERBY

TOP SPEED: Disappointingly slow

0–60 MPH (0-97 KM/H) : Never gets that fast

HORSEPOWER: From 100 bhp upward

LENGTH: Varies from car to car

WIDTH: Varies from car to car

HEIGHT: Varies from car to car

MADE IN: Various countries

MINI ALL4 RACING

The Mini All4 Racing is one of the toughest supercars in the world. This was proved when it won the world's harshest race—the Dakar. To do this, the Mini had to endure all types of harsh driving conditions, from rugged mountains to sweltering deserts, and most of the time the car was off road or following rough tracks. Not only did the Mini do it, but it did it better than anyone else!

The rear seats have been removed, which gives a bigger storage area; handy, as the racers need lots of extra gear—including the three spare tires.

The rear brakes are cooled by jets of water to stop them overheating. If brakes get too hot, they stop working as they should, which would be really bad news!

The tires were specially designed for the Dakar race and have to be tough enough to survive all sorts of different road surfaces.

The body is made from carbon fiber and is designed so that most parts can be quickly removed and replaced if they get damaged.

In 2013 the Mini won the Dakar, a difficult route that went from Peru into Argentina and finished in Chile. The race was more than 5,000 miles (8,000 km) long and lasted for two weeks. Some race days stretched more than 500 miles (800 km). The Mini had to get over the Andes Mountains and survive the Atacama Desert—the driest place on Earth!

Around half the entrants to the Dakar don't finish as the race is so tough on both drivers and their cars.

Unlike most types of race car, the All4 is powered by a diesel engine, which is well-suited for hard, long-distance races such as the Dakar.

The Mini needs as much grip as possible, so the way the air flows over the spoilers is really important as this pushes the car down on to the ground.

SUPER STATS

MINI ALL4 RACING

TOP SPEED: Around 111 mph (178 km/h)

0–60 MPH (0-97 KM/H): Top secret

HORSEPOWER: 307 bhp

LENGTH: 170.5 in (4,333 mm)

WIDTH: 78.6 in (1,998 mm)

HEIGHT: 78.5 in (1,996 mm)

MADE IN: Great Britain

MEAN MACHINES

AUDI R18 E-TRON QUATTRO

The Audi R18 e-tron quattro is arguably one of the most important and impressive racing cars around today. Not only did it win the prestigious Le Mans 24 Hour race, but it achieved this using hybrid technology, proving that part-electric cars can perform as well as—if not better than—normally fueled racers!

The R18 is an endurance racer, which means it takes part in competitions that can last for up to 24 hours. That's tough going for any car.

Every time the Audi driver steps on the brakes, the car stores the energy generated as it slows down. It then uses this energy to power the front wheels.

There are strict rules on how much each racing car can weigh. Having an electric motor and an engine adds weight, so the R18 has a new lightweight engine to stop the car being too heavy.

What makes the Audi so special is that it uses a gasoline engine to power the rear wheels and an electric motor to drive the front ones. This hybrid technology is available in family cars, but they tend to be slow and heavy. The R18 has proved that if it's done well it can be a benefit and not a burden!

The wheels are made from magnesium, which is lighter than steel but strong.

The body is made from one single piece of carbon fiber called a monocoque.

Front view cameras increase the driver's view of what's ahead of him by displaying the images in the cockpit.

SUPER STATS

AUDI R18 E-TRON QUATTRO
TOP SPEED: Around 200 mph (320 km/h)
0–60 MPH (0-97 KM/H) : Top secret
HORSEPOWER: Over 490 bhp
LENGTH: 183 in (4,650 mm)
WIDTH: 78.7 in (2,000 mm)
HEIGHT: 40.5 in (1,030 mm)
MADE IN: Germany

CITROËN 2CV

The Citroën 2CV is quite possibly the ultimate racing car. This might sound surprising, as the 2CV hasn't been made for decades. Also, it's slow, has thin wheels and an underpowered engine. However, no other car competes in as many different types of racing as the 2CV. It has taken part in road races, track competitions, rallies, 24-hour races, and even the Dakar!

The 2CV is a very basic car. There are no electric windows, for example—in fact there aren't even wind-up windows! If you want to open the window you have to fold it up!

The body of the car is incredibly light thanks to the thin steel it's made from. This makes it perfect for driving over soft ground.

The 2CV was first made in the 1940s and was designed for people living in the country. The idea was that you could fit a sheep in the back and that the ride would be smooth enough to carry a basket of eggs over a bumpy field without breaking any. No one imagined it was a racing car, but the combination of lightness and excellent suspension made it exactly that!

2CVs don't have a radiator to cool the engine like most cars—instead they use air.

The speedometer on a 2CV only goes up to 70 mph (112 km/h), but it can go faster—especially downhill with the wind behind it.

2CVs are nicknamed "tin snails" thanks to their distinctive shape and less than amazing speeds.

SUPER STATS

CITROËN 2CV

TOP SPEED: Around 90 mph (144 km/h)

0–60 MPH (0-97 KM/H) : 35 (yes, thirty-five!) seconds

HORSEPOWER: 29 bhp

LENGTH: 150.7 in (3,828 mm)

WIDTH: 58.2 in (1,478 mm)

HEIGHT: 62.9 in (1,598 mm)

MADE IN: France

GLOSSARY

aerodynamic Designed to move through the air easily.

bhp This stands for "brake horsepower" and is the measurement of the power of an engine.

carbon fiber A thin, strong material which is made from rods of carbon. Carbon is also found in coal and diamonds.

cockpit The space in a racing car (or aircraft) where the driver sits.

cowling A metal covering that protects the engine of a vehicle.

friction A force that resists motion between two objects.

hybrid car A car that uses two or more power sources.

nitromethane An organic compound used as a racing fuel in Top Fuel drag racing.

roll cage A frame built into the passenger compartment in a vehicle to protect the occupants from being injured in a crash.

spoiler A device fitted to the rear of a vehicle, designed to help improve the airflow over the car and increase its speed.

tubular Long, round and hollow; shaped like a tube.

FURTHER READING

Christopher, Matt. *Great Moments in American Auto Racing.* Little, Brown Books for Younger Readers, 2011.

Kelley, K. C. *Hottest NASCAR Machines.* Enslow Publishing, 2009.

McClurg, Bob. *Diggers, Funnies, Gassers, and Altereds: Drag Racing's Golden Age.* Car Tech, 2013.

INDEX